I'LL LET YOU
TASTE MY WINE
IF I
CAN TASTE YOURS

I'LL LET YOU
TASTE MY WINE

IF I
CAN TASTE YOURS

Edited by
R. Paul Firnhaber

Concordia Publishing House
St. Louis   London

Published by
Concordia Publishing House, St. Louis, Missouri
Concordia Publishing House Ltd., London, E. C. 1
© 1969 Walther League
Library of Congress Catalog Card No. 77-77627

MANUFACTURED IN THE UNITED STATES OF AMERICA

PREFACE

These intimate and personal letters (some only excerpts) were written over the past several years by young people ranging in age from 13 to perhaps 22. Except for change of names and places, they were only slightly edited for readability.

The writers had one thing in common: all had chosen to leave for a time the comfortable familiarity of home, community, family, and friends and spend a time in the unfamiliar world of a country, society, city, or community different from their own. Almost all were involving themselves in volunteer or exchange programs sponsored by the church. This may make their expressions uncommon, but I don't think so.

The letters were obviously not written for publication. Had they been written for publication —to inform, to entertain, or to please—they would without doubt be less honest than they are. But since they are segments of postal dialogs between themselves and friends they loved, families they missed, or adults they trusted, they reflect a candidness and honesty not often expressed publicly or captured in print.

They might scare you. They might confuse you. They might threaten you. They might anger you. They might please you. Depending, of course, on who you are. It would be unthinkable for you to agree with every thought or feeling expressed here. It wouldn't be fair to ask that of you, nor would it be fair for you to approach them judgmentally, because you are getting just a few minutes' slice of a person's life and thoughts. You don't know the experiences, the anguish, the joy, the struggle that led to this moment's expression. You can't see the writer's face. You don't know who he is. You don't know his history.

Maybe it's too much to expect of you, to listen to such a tiny piece of a person. But perhaps that's what the book is about. Because in knowing no more about these people than you do, you are forced to see yourself in their place, or perhaps a person you know. In fact, the time you spend with this parade of people might well provide you a necessary exercise in listening to people on their own terms, accepting people where they are, loving people when you don't understand them, concerning yourself about people when you can't see their faces.

We hope you will listen, but not just with patience and understanding. Listen also with anticipation and openness. These are Christian young people straining to express the faith, forgiveness, and love Christ has given them. They are committed to their incarnate Lord in a total, deep, and radical way. They are struggling with their entire existence with the issue of what it means to be a Christian in a world that doesn't easily let them express their love and concern. They are shaping out of precious little raw material a style of Christian existence that includes rather than excludes the brother in need. They are attacking at an early age societal ills from which most of us successfully insulate ourselves for an entire lifetime. They are idealistic, but at the same time realistic.

They hope and at the same time cry. They work and at the same time laugh and sing. They are saints and at the same time sinners. They want change and at the same time respect their heritage. They are totally human. And they have much to offer you.

But their offering is not for everyone. The title itself creates an exclusive readership. Taken from one of the letters, it demands that only those who are willing to be as free and honest about their persons, their feelings, their doubts, their struggles, their joys, their God, their world as they, should dare to enter into the dialog created here. For its pages evolved out of a community of concern, and only those willing to share freely in that unique community should read past this period.

R. PAUL FIRNHABER

1

I can hardly wait for summertime. I'm sick of school. It just seems like a waste of time; besides, it's boring. I just can't get excited about learning anymore. Like the only part I really enjoy are the basketball games and swimming meets.

Have you ever met one of those sugary sweet persons who, to me, sound like complete fakes? I've been studying the Bible. It tells you to sympathize, to try to keep peace, etc. I honestly don't care about very many people. I also don't care what they think of me either. When I try to care about a person like this, I feel I'm being sugary sweet and worse than that, an utter fake. Why is it I could honestly love the group of kids this summer? Why is it I can't care about another group of human beings, just like the kids this summer, with bad points and good points? Is it that I'm two-faced, a person who acts like a good Christian girl one place and an uncaring, hateful person at another? Or is it the kids themselves? Can a group of kids who can proudly say, "We're Christians," be that different from others? God, I want to be good so badly, I want to be like them. How can I ever hope to be good when I continually fall so short of the mark?

Church is church. I keep my mouth shut in front of the pastor and teach and think what I think's right. But I'm very seriously thinking of nicely voicing my opinion at the next teachers' meeting.

I must close. I've got a million silly things to do imposed on me because of my age and the society which I'm stuck living in.

2

After a couple of weeks of questioning motives and feelings, I've decided that if the Lord doesn't do something to change my mind, I'm going to drop out of college for a year. There are several reasons which have molded my thinking: this semester I've been trying to balance my time between studies and other constructive things, such as entering into relationships and just generally living in the joy of atonement with Him. Many times I've found myself analyzing situations concerning people, and then worrying about their solutions. In talking with friends it's apparent that I've been playing God and then feeling frustration when I couldn't make the grade.

My grades aren't bad; in fact they may be very good. However, I've felt uneasy and restless several times, usually while studying, and don't seem to be very stable in my situation. My pastor has freed me from excessive worry about school, so my present effort has been to do my best without worrying about it.

Something may happen to alter my decision. If it does, that will be great. All I know now is that life can be great and beautiful, but I seem to be out of it.

This letter may sound very confusing, but sometimes it's tough to explain why you feel moved to do a certain thing.

Please let me know what you think.

PS. My parents don't know my intentions as of yet. I'm not sure what their reaction will be.

3

4

Such a weekend. Such thrills. There's nothing like a sprint to the center, which was not so good for my messed-up knee.

I wanna go to school. I'm lonely. I want something to hold on to. I'm tired of using my music for my only joy and company.

Sure I got Willie, but it seems he's never around.

I know you're gonna tell me I got God, and he is always with me, but I can't reach out and touch him. I try to pray, and my mind wanders, and I end up forgetting what I set out to do.

My brother, mom, and I are always fighting. She's mad at him, so she's mad at me.

I want out so bad it hurts. I don't want to go home. They're always fighting. I'm a wreck. I don't find comfort in anything.

I'm tired of being in the middle of fights. I'm tired of being alone at night. I'm tired of yelling. I'm tired of being lonely.

It's no use.

5

When we first came to Japan, I was very relaxed. I didn't get shook up or get bugged for a long time. I slept well and woke up each morning open to the day to come, to whatever new sights and sounds it might bring. But one day at language school the whole thing blew up. I let something bother me. That day I realized what hangups are. Hangups are people. When I came here, I left the old people behind, and the things about them and me that did not jive too well. But as I got to know my new associates, the Japanese instructors, etc., new points of tension began to build. Soon everything was back to "normal." Let's face it; people, even Christians, don't "love their neighbor as themselves." I guess we have to learn to accept this. To expect nothing, to accept reproach with humility. This must be "turning the other cheek." I read an article comparing Zen Buddhism and Quakerism. It said, "Christians are good at preaching brotherly love." This is fine, but what do you do when you don't love your brother anyway? How do you survive in the actual situation?

The other night Jack and I went to a Good-bye (for Jack)—Welcome (me)—House-warming (one of the teachers) party with the English faculty of one of the schools here in Asahigawa where Jack had been teaching and where I will be teaching. These sorts of things are rather nervous events for me at best. But I thought I was doing quite well, throwing in a jovial comment or story here and there, and they seemed to enjoy it, and I was quite relaxed and content. But at the end the department head said that although they wouldn't see Jack at school anymore they hoped we could all meet from time to time although "Mr. Davis doesn't seem to enjoy our company too much." So it all comes rushing back. Bitterness and frustration. Up go the defenses. Who is at fault? They are, for chiding me for not being the life of the party, for in doing this they are only pointing out their own ill-at-easeness, their discomfort at not having it covered by someone else's relaxed and easy manner. I am at fault, for not being what they expected, but for letting their mild reproach bother me. For not being humble, for not turning the other cheek. For nursing my bitterness. Naive people don't know when they are insulted. Bitter, hard-bitten people know. Strong people know but can bear it graciously. So their strength is often mistaken for naivete. We admire the openness of children. But to be an open adult means we must let a lot of junk in too. Let in the good, and the bad comes in too. Shut out the bad, and you shut out the good too. So I think I should not try to be the life of the party but try to accept graciously the fact that others may reproach me for not being what they expected me to be. To remain open to them. So I am trying to do something—what?

Maybe I want to develop my style of being a Christian. There, of course, are proper styles for various Christian callings. Ministers, of course, are "shepherds of the flock," "followers of the highest calling," etc., etc. Youth workers are wildly optimistic, horribly enthusiastic. What Christ means to them, and how it has "changed their lives," just oozes out of their ears. Naturally there are good singers and musicians too. "Ah, what a grand sight, to see a young person using his talents for Christ!" The point is that they would be outgoing, likable, and talented persons whether they were Christians or not. I remember two girls back home. Judi, she is genuinely outgoing, likable, and talented, the traditional Christian style is her style. Then I remember Mary, another person with style — warm, outgoing, able to sacrifice, aware of things as they are, able to move freely among people. But outside the church (although, I suspect, not outside Christ).

Well, my talent is skiing, not singing; a way with things, not people. I must develop my Christian style around what I am, not what other people expect Christians to be.

6

Where do I start? I guess I should say that I'm terribly alive. God, I hurt, but I want to hurt more. I want to go. I want to see. I want to feel. I love it. I love life. Every single bit of it. The challenge. O Lord, the overpowering challenge, the pain, the overwhelming giddiness and spasticness that hits you for no reason. I hate it. The unfairness, the selfishness, the insensitivity, the cruelness, the ignorance. I feel alive. God help me. I've got to let go. It's like taking off, like taking a flying leap off this earth and frantically clawing at those white cotton clouds that are supposed to be heaven. But if you can only get a handful of those clouds, clutching it in your hands and sticking it between your breasts. It's always there. It scratches at times. Sometimes you have to touch it to make sure it's there. You forget about it. And sometimes it fills your body with a warmth like a wool blanket gives you. I feel wonderful. I just remembered what a pastor said last night. "Beware of the man whose God is in heaven." He's here. Sticking pins in us, while at the same time caressing the spasmed muscles of our neck. I'm caught. I don't know where I'm going, how things are going to turn out, but I'm a fly in a spider's web, stuck full of strands of glue, reaching out for more strands to wrap my pain with.

Maybe you don't know what I'm talking about. I don't even know if I do. But, good God, Jim doesn't matter, my parents don't matter. As God's children caught in a relationship, we count. But as idiotic lizards, we don't mean a thing.

7

Let me tell you where I am at 3:45 this afternoon: I am caught between working in the system (I had to transfer churches because they tried to put me in a box and the only thing left for me to do was scream, but I got sick of that game and needed a church where I was free to give and free to take, so I'm a member at another church now—here I can be a human being) and just taking off for a hippie colony or moving to Watts and working as a person (green, not black or white) and mostly just being and living. It's probably because I am very frustrated just now, discouraged and disgusted. Is there a kind of place within the church where I could be a human being with other human beings and not get busted for it?

8

It was a fantastic summer — with many awakenings, rude as some were. It was something that touched my heart in a way — I'm sure it will always stay with me.

It's so hard to explain myself — but I guess I'm just reaching so high — in hopes of finding that which will make life.

9

Though the importance of the "being" sometimes becomes questionable in our minds, there are always some terrific moments that leave us without a doubt. One such incident happened last week on the way to school. On a playground a little boy was sprawled out on the concrete with his two playmates looking anxiously over him. Investigating the matter at close range, I found the fallen one to be only a bit scratched and a bit more shaken. After a moment, he stopped crying and we helped him to his feet. Seeing that there was nothing to be done, I told the boys "bye" and went on my way as they went theirs. After I had gone about 20 paces, one of the little guys turned around and said, "Hey, lady, you're nice!" That made my day!

11

From Tokyo Jerry and I split up, and we hitchhiked back to Sapporo (about the distance from New York to St. Louis or New Orleans). Jerry had to hurry back, but I dawdled my way, stopping wherever I wanted to. My Japanese was getting fairly good before I left, but it really grew up on that trip. I had a ride from a communist youth organizer, and we spent about five hours talking about the mystery of time and what lies behind it. I even picked up a hitchhiking buddy on the way, a nineteen-year-old high school student who had been heading for Tokyo but decided to switch directions to travel with me. I even met a few Japanese Christians on the way (most of them very doubtful about it all) and had the pleasure of seeing that one of them at least sees something more behind it all than a God-of-the-Glad-Hand.

I have not decided whether I am in love with Japan or the world. But I beam with joy, joy! Hunger, ever, always, hungry! Gadzooks, is being alive a groove!!

The meeting I was heading for was a comedown. Yeah, there were a lot of guys and girls at this here meeting, you see, and we sat around praising a pedantic, faded godhead in a stuffy room for five (5!) days, amid the gray rustle, the death rattle of a myriad of prematurely bald ideas. Meanwhile, outside, nature was peeling herself open in an ecstasy of cherry blossoms, the God of Life was beating on the windows, banging on the doorsill. But then we were much too busy for all of that.

12

I have tried and tried to write to you to give you some sort of advice, but I can't tell you what you should do. I can only say what I plan to do in the future for as long as it takes to bring love and understanding not only between our races but all people. First let me tell you something important. I am slowly but surely turning more and more militant. I am finding it difficult to be friendly with whites primarily because so many of the people I know at school that are white are true hypocrites. Our school is known for its equality and liberalism, yet one teacher didn't know there was a difference between a nigger and a Negro. He also said that he accepted me and that I was different than other blacks. He was able to accept me because I was a white black man. This is where I must start within myself. I must find the "truth." I have to lose all my false airs and be black if that is what I am or be white if that is what I am. I would prefer not to make that choice because I would rather be thought of as even. But the kids at school need black people to help them lose their sickness just as black people at school need whites to help end all of the fears and prejudice their parents and society put into them. While I am talking about parents—often kids at school say, "Oh, I like Negroes, but my parents don't like me to go to the south side." True, very often parents do lead their children into prejudice and fear of blacks, but also remember most kids have reason. And if reason told them, as it should, that their parents are wrong, and they should associate with Negroes, everything would be fine. But for the most part they don't. The kids at school for the most part are following in their parents' footsteps of prejudice, and what's terrible about it is that they don't admit it. At least their parents do, some of them. But then again a good deal of the parents just smile at you with a phony smile and bat their eyelashes and breathe like something in the room smelled bad. Perhaps you know of this, maybe you don't. Oh, the stories I could tell you would make you vomit. I wish I could tell you some of the insults I and my parents have received. But I can't. I asked one of my friends if he would marry a Negro. He said, "No!" I then said, "Not even if you loved her?" He said, "What? Are you crazy? Get out of here with such nonsense." This was a best friend. He said this to my face. I could give you millions of incidents. And you know, I'm finding it hard not to hate that guy.

I feel sorry for you because you, like other "good whites," will be hurt unless we can change the situation in the country. And don't think you can't do anything; because it is up to people like you to do it, because no one else will do it. Blacks are finding it difficult to rap to whites about "the problem" because the whites, like everyone else, need to be pushed and pushed and the black man is losing his patience. He can't push with hate. It takes love that only people like you can give. So all I can really say to you is do it in your own way, but do something even if it is just rapping to two or three people, your parents, anyone. If you have any other questions to ask, I don't know if I could help you with them, but all I can do is try like anyone. Thank you very much for writing me. Your happiness is in my prayers, and continue to be white and beautiful.

13

14

North Dakota is undecided about me. No one's sure if I'm just a liberal nut, a radical, or more likely a communist. The reactions wouldn't have surprised me so much if I had voiced any opinions, because here anything that isn't conservative is radical. But I haven't even said anything yet.

My mother really shocked me. I've always been taught to take an active part in things and to stand up for what I believe in. Now suddenly it's alright to be involved as long as I don't get all radical about it. Mom is firmly convinced that I have been duped by the Reds. I just don't realize it because "they" are so clever and I'm so young. Every other minute she says she is sure the communists will take over by 1970, now that even her daughter has joined "them." I feel sorry for her.

Mom has always used the Bible to prove she is right. I have heard Romans 13 so often in the past few days that I think I say it in my sleep. When I try to present my side, I'm disobeying the Fourth Commandment.

School started out bad. Being I didn't actually get into the convention, they didn't feel I could use that as an excuse for being late. Then I got to my American Problems class and found out that 98% voted in support of the police action during the convention. My instructor asked me to tell the class about Michigan Avenue. I told them what I saw with no other comments. Most of the kids were shocked by what I said, but they still felt the brutality was probably necessary to control the "riots." The instructor reminded everyone that an eyewitness account is not always as accurate as it would seem, especially when given by someone young and impressionable. Most of the kids were a lot more concerned about me being in a Peace March than anything else. If I have to be disloyal, I should have the sense to be quiet about it. Marching proves I'm a traitor. They just look at me and shake their heads. And I haven't even said anything.

I am also overly sympathetic with "colored people." Some of the comments people have made are unreal. Some of the questions are cool too, like, "Was it really depressing trying to help people that are by nature so lazy and dirty?" And most often, "Was it really beautiful in the slums helping all the poor people?" I haven't said much. I was hoping they'd listen to what they were saying. Once I used one of Jim's lines and asked what color they were talking about. That, of course, reaffirmed that I am a radical.

I guess I shouldn't sound so disillusioned so early. You told us that we shouldn't feel alone, because we'd find others to work with us. My problem is, I'm really not sure how to approach people. I know that last year I would have been hard to talk to, and probably would have some of the same arguments.

15

In these times of racial whirlwinds, you and your family gleam like a "cluster of jewels in the mud." You and your family should be duplicated 100,000-fold, then maybe we could head off the approaching cloud of doom.

I have often thought of you Christians because I have seen and heard many white folks pay lip service to the words of "loyalty, support," and if I may, "struggle." Unfortunately, though, few stick around after the crusade becomes a crisis.

Funny thing: when I was viewing the whole Kennedy scene, I could not help but think of Huey and Elridge, Rap, Resurrection City, and we six. It all seemed like death. I thought, the flags have always flown half mast for us and will.

I have been asking for 8½×14 yellow legal pads to start writing a few notes about all this for nearly a month and ten days. It seems those spineless, spermless so-called peddlers of spirits cannot even bring paper.

I am reasonably sure of release next week. There are some important things I wish to discuss with you. Tell you what! Dinner is on me when we hit ground.

I gather from your letter that you are concerned about our "spirits." We are keeping the faith, grinning and bearing it. I would not give "them" the satisfaction of discouraging and destroying me short of death.

17

Lots of disillusionment — negative thoughts right now. Especially about the whole church and Jesus bit. Many serious questions there.

True, this is one of the most progressive churches (forced to belong to any other, I'd get out immediately), but the religious bit here is even too much at times.

I'm completely up in the air about summer and about my future here. Right now I feel I want to chuck it because I can't go along with the religious bit at all.

Got all kinds of thoughts about getting out of this country and bumming — traveling and drawing and meeting people — (some would call it a cop-out, or an escape; I don't care).

Also this Easter I want to get away from it all — to write, think, paint, and sketch. I want nothing of my home, relatives, or friends. Got any suggestions as to what I can do? or where I can go? I'm willing to fly (it's cheap!).

18

I know I'm kidding myself when I say I'm going to leave all institution and organization. But I say it anyway, mainly because I blow things out of proportion when I get upset, and suddenly all institutions exist to be served instead of to serve. 1 Corinthians 4 is beautiful. It has a lot of things to say, and I think I understand it. That one thing you said—our worth doesn't depend on how we do or don't feel about God—struck me and gave me some sort of comfort. It was kind of funny.

But the things you said in your letter, for the most, applied more to something else than the fact that at the time I wrote to you I was just about ready to take off for the redwoods and some commune someplace. And I'm not going to be very coherent, I'm sure. You see, I run around with this Vietnam peace symbol on me, and my brother (who isn't related to me—we just grew up together, and I've been his little sister) suddenly turned friend and lover last Saturday, and he left for Vietnam Monday morning for thirteen months.

Now that makes for all kinds of confusion. First of all, the change in relationship, which I still can't quite believe happened (I feel all those different things toward him, and they haven't melted together yet), and then the fact that he's in Vietnam, he understands why we're there (which I'm beginning to after his explanation, which he could never have given in uniform), but I just somehow can't justify any of it. And of course Jerry's relationship with God is only an acknowledgment of the probability of God; thank God He has a relationship with Jerry anyhow. So anyhow, I get my brain blown out of my head, and I've been numb with feeling since Saturday, and I'm starting to recover.

19

We've got the most beautiful friendship, and it would hurt more than anything I can imagine for him to die right now, or for a long time. But I'm especially confronted with the possibility right now (he's a helicopter pilot) that he may get killed. We've been separated for years before, but death is kind of final. It's like the last experience of life, and he's only 22 (his birthday was Tuesday — why does the Army always do that, send people away on some important time? Oh, well). The whole thing blew my brain.

And your letter and the things you said about God and about man and about me somehow gave me a little peace, but I can't explain it. I'm just all jazzed up that somehow because of something a Man, the Son of God, did 2,000 years ago I can write to you like this. And you can understand and accept. That's the grooviest thing. That you accept all the stuff I've been throwing at you since Easter, that someplace you accepted me. And I know that's not an easy thing. I do not go to pains to be acceptable. I do go to pains to be real, though, and sometimes that results in selfish honesty and sometimes in taking myself too seriously, and sometimes it results in reality. That's like sometimes I make *being* the goal, and blow the whole thing, ego trip like, and that always brings a crash. Yeah, and what you said: we are free to scream or not to scream.

And we don't have to prove anything, because it doesn't matter, we're free. What you said about the need to gather together, 2 or 3, yeah, O. K. That's vital, I understand. We're not part of the church, we are the church—ah, beautiful. Complications, problems, you know, sin. I think freedom which we have, given freely to us, not on anything we ever did or felt or thought, is the hardest thing to accept. And it's hard to keep it accepted, if you understand what I'm talking about, which is difficult, because I'm never too coherent. What you said, apart from the Word that frees you, you would have to run and turn black when you're white. From some friends and some thoughts I have been starting to feel that, and I can't quite (and there's no word, of course, for what I can't quite—someplace between internalize and comprehend and realize and feel totally) yet, but I've got the distant sensation that's going to be a flash pretty soon. Maybe God doesn't come off logical sometimes because He FEELS. I don't know how that occurred to me just now.

20

Knowingly or unknowingly the university is producing young men and women who are well educated and will act intelligently in society, with the same indifference that one would expect from a machine. Must religion be a thing of the intellect, as complicated as the rest of modern society? Whatever happened to human kindness and compassion, what has happened to the things that come from the heart, not the mind? Maybe I'm just a plain old southwesterner, small-town boy who shudders at the thought of the direction in which the world is proceeding, but I would sincerely hate to live in the world which my children will someday live in. I suppose that someday people will never know what life really is, at least what I think it is.

22

I can't see how it's possible. If I shut
my eyes to what's happening, I shouldn't be
here, and if I don't, how can I make it through
school?

Anxious to get working on a four-hour
assignment yesterday, I didn't see the urgent
need of a young girl who had just been attacked
on the way home from school. I blindly labeled
it as one of her moods and went about *my*
business. I feel so lousy about it, and through
this I can see where I have neglected other
people — such as the rest of the kids here.

I try not to shut the door in their faces
if I can tell that they need someone to talk to.
I need them to come to me, too, but some
things gotta give.

I don't know — it's so hard. Everything just
collapsed tonight when I heard about this girl.
I don't know how to be helped, either.

23

I really don't know why I decided at this
moment to write you. I've been putting off this
letter for so long that I wonder what crisis
must be going on inside me to pick up this pen
and write. Maybe because I have never felt
farther away from this summer. It seems as if the
summer was a totally unrealistic dream world.
Now, looking back, I can almost trace the steps
of me gradually coming farther and farther away

from my dream. Every once in a while I get this terrific reoccurrence of last summer. I feel guilty, but I deftly push my feelings under with thoughts of school and all the "important" little things on my mind. Dramatic as it sounds, at times I'm beyond feelings, and other times I am so overcome with feelings, I think that I will split. Right now I am depressed. I could name off 20 things that need to be done, but somehow I just can't start. I feel that I'm missing something important, but I can't put my finger on it. I feel so lost and alone.

24

Integrated a movie theater and drive-in with some of our older kids last week. Got called "white trash" and spit on by the ticket taker, but after a while we ended up having a private showing of the movie. Everybody else left. They will tolerate Negro patronage at most places, but it's the mixed groups which turn them off. They'll just have to get used to it. This business takes mainly a generous amount of guts and a sense of humor, but too much of it I can't take.

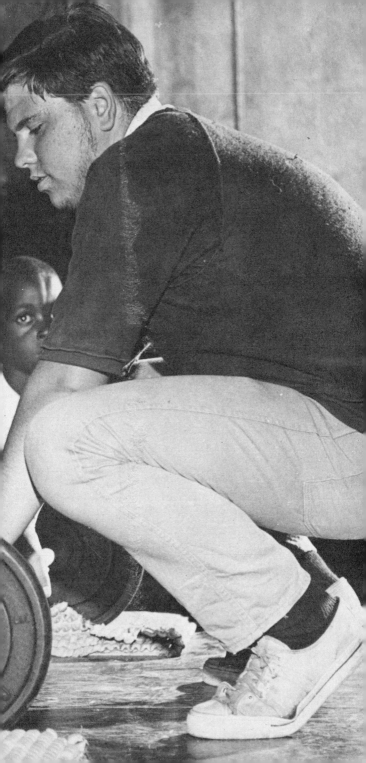

26

There is absolutely no one in this world
but me. I, alone, have to arrive at the conclusion
of what I am. I've tried being a Christian. I hate
too many people for that. Sometimes I pray so
hard that I cry. I feel nothing. I have never
felt an answer. Gone is my inner calm. To
replace it is doubt. I have never felt like such a
hypocrite. I would worship God in a minute if
only I could feel that somehow He was near me,
help me and caring about me.

I look at my parents. They are people I am
supposed to love. I guess I love them, but
I neither respect, admire, or like them. The first
thing I think of when I see them is their faults.
I want to get out of this home, this school,
this world so badly that it hurts. I despise a weak
escapist, but that is how I feel. I'm trying to be
truthful, but since I've been lying so long, lies
are creeping into my words. Sometimes I can't
tell when I lie and when I'm telling the truth.
I'm plagued with so many questions and so much
confusion, I don't know which way to turn.

The day is sunny, and a little bluish bird is
flying around. Just this picture-thought lets things
come a little clearer, but my heart seems to be
developing a hard spot in the middle. Please
don't get upset about me. I fully intend on getting
a grand flash and becoming a strong and steadfast
Christian. I'm partly lying. I do want someone to
care about me. I've looked for it in guys, but
I always come out unsatisfied. I still want a guy
badly. I'm almost ready to settle for something
less than what I want.

Do you really feel something after a prayer? How many times have I prayed, "O Lord, I can't do it alone; help me." I never get the peace of mind I'm supposed to. Where have I gone wrong? What can I do? Where is God? Why doesn't He give me just a tiny bit of help? Why do I have to suffer and suffer? I've had enough mental anguish for my 15 years. When are the returns going to start coming in? How much longer can I wait? I think it was Emily Dickinson that said, "I know I must go on living, but I wonder why."

At this moment, as honestly as I can tell, this is the way I feel. I still laugh and have fun, but I am never entirely happy. I must solve my own problems, but I had to talk to someone I know who can understand my pain.

27

Larry was invited by me this summer to come to my house for a few days during the holiday. Well, as you know, my parents aren't going to jump for joy over this prospect and have even hinted that he better not come. Okay, fine, but what on earth do I do now? I want to see him; he's my friend as well as the precious white ones. I'd just go ahead and have him come on to the house, but I'm afraid that he might really get hurt and wouldn't want that for the world. Maybe I'm trying to protect myself, too, I don't know. Liz suggested that I go to Memphis, which I'd like, but that wouldn't help the lousy situation at home any. When I'm faced with something like this, my eyes immediately go to a verse I have above my desk. It says, "We shall have all

eternity in which to rest, now let us work."
I want to work and truly make "the world
a better place," but HOW? Janie kind of
summed this up when she said that she has
discovered that we should simply "love as He
first loved us." I suppose this is true, especially
when I compare loving, real love, with concrete
jobs. It's a heck of a lot harder to truly love
than it is to perform menial tasks. I've learned
just recently that this love can take on many
forms, even to the extent of being rude to
someone. Now I can see that God's love can't
always be the wonderful things that happened
to us throughout our lives, but also has to be
the mean, cruel things that happen to help
along the way.

28

When I left this area, there was a lot of
soul searching since one year here had proven
that it was only enough time to almost get
myself settled and accepted and started working
to a certain point. And then to leave was like
saying to my friends, "Thanks for the
experience, but now I've got to move on.
Thanks for the trust and love you had for me.
Thanks for the hope and growth you had—
and even though you had a taste of the hope
in yourself but aren't yet strong enough to go
for yourself—well, better luck next time."
     This was brought vividly home to me when
the greatest teacher I ever had (an artist who
died over a year ago from cancer) said, "Kitten,
the people here love and trust you. They know
you've got a lot to give. The kids see you as
someone who can and has taught them about

this whole sick and beautiful life. You don't play games with us—you're truthful. You've given them a taste, but you don't have guts enough to stay until they get on their own two feet. You're like the rest of the do-gooders—you're going to drop them; and believe me, they're going to be worse off than before. Who do you think you are?"

The more I see, the more I realize the truth of his statement. Like, man, if you're going to do a job and be a person, you've got to go all the way—or don't get involved in the first place. It's not enough to go into something like this because it's an adventure or an unusual experience you can grow from—because you end up harming rather than helping the people that just might need you an awful lot. I'm not saying it's wrong to grow, but maybe we're defeating ourselves if we don't realize the position of the other person.

So my third Christmas in New York is one of many joys and sorrows but most of all one of life and love.

It means a phone call from a sobbing 15-year-old. "Sue, I've got V. D., and I don't know what to do."

It means a stone junkie letting out a war whoop because I'm there again.

It means a Black Muslim calling me "sister."

It means the joy of a 16-year-old experiencing her first Christmas.

It means collard greens, rice and beans and beef stew all mixed together with spaghetti.

It means a Monday night girls' group meeting when two archenemies make up for the first time in 3 years.

It means all the wheres and hows and

whys of life wrapped in packages of all different sizes and shapes and colors.

And it means those few precious minutes alone with the one I love.

It's that simple, wonderful knowledge within of the joy of living.

I wish a truthful Christmas and new year to you.

30

My last days in South America were enjoyable, and even more so was the month I spent in Mexico. I lived on a beach about twenty miles north of Acapulco with a fisherman and his family. I paid $1.40 a day for a hammock on the beach and three beautiful fish dinners a day. Could his wife cook! Fished, lay in the hammock and drank tequila, and swam when the sun got too hot. If I didn't run out of money, I would still be down there. One knows or cares less about Bigger and Better Bombs for world peace, smaller but more powerful bombs for blowing up colored people, or some Oriental fink who preaches that even if 400,000,000 of his people did get the brains blown out of them, there would still be 300,000,000 to spread his way of thinking to the world. Of course it's an escapist attitude, why not.

It's great to be back here in the land of opportunity, where people throw bombs under churches which blow apart little colored people. But the great American public forgets in the din of Sandy Koufax winning the world series for the Dodgers. No, I'm not crusading. I'm losing myself in the problems of the Holy Alliance of 1815 and American imperialism in 1989 here at the university — much simpler. Albuquerque is nice, the climate swings, and politically it's not the cancer I thought it would be.

31

I hardly know where to begin. Many
sights have passed before my eyes, many
sounds my ears, many experiences have had to
be grasped, coped with, and either understood
or not understood since I last saw you. Life
was thrown in my face in every respect every
time I turned around. I sometimes thought that
I would never be able to survive — that I was
drowning in an unescapable sea. I ran. Perhaps
I am still running — running from a way of life
that I can't accept; searching for one I can
accept; searching for happiness. But it is my
search. I have to make it. There is a possibility
that no one will ever be able to understand.
There is also a possibility that I will destroy
the relationships I have had since birth, a
possibility I will destroy even myself. The
chances are mine, and I am taking them.

I have resigned my position here for two
main reasons and many, many lesser ones.
The most important reason was my own
inadequacy, and my feeling that everything that
I was doing as a job should and would have to
be done as a part of my life every day of my
life for the rest of my life. The second important
reason was my changing feeling about what part
I could and should play in the racial issue.
I discovered while working with Negroes in
the South that my place as I see it is not working
with them but rather talking with people that
I come in contact with every day, preparing
them for what is to come, breaking down old
prejudices, fears, tales — perhaps in such small
ways as telling one of my girl friends that

Negroes don't smell any different than whites.
The Negro in America today is a member of the
important race. The spotlight is on him. What
happens now will have an effect on the future,
the times to come, the generations to come.
Now is the time. The stage is set. The acting
must, however, be done by real people, not by
actors with paint on their faces.

I realize that I am a disappointment, but
I am not a failure, because I am still fighting for
life. I have resigned my post here, but I will
never be able to resign as a special kind of
person, for that post was given to me at my
baptism; I stated my desire to keep it at my
confirmation, and this post I shall have until
I die.

I pray that in some small way you will
understand me. I am a person; I am Ruth
Downing; I exist; I must find a reason for
this existence, and a way of existence. I can no
longer hide behind anyone or anything. If I fall,
at least I will know that I was doing what I felt
I had to do to maintain my integrity, at least
I won't fall a complete coward.

I ask not for your forgiveness but rather for
your understanding and your blessing.

32

it's a crisp, bright autumn day and as i crane
my neck i can see from my study window
a swath of orange, brown red and green: the
duller browns mute the brighter reds and while
i know there is something profound about that,
about the whole business of autumn (death
wishes; maybe even the necessity of dying in
order to be born again; the wonder and glory of
death; died in full; dyed in fullness), i'm too sick
to make any profound connections even though
one of my favorite authors, john updike, wrote
a nice poem once about the profound truths that
are revealed in sickness: "I have brought back
a message from the land of 102° — God exists" —
or words to that effect. look up the poem
sometime; it is in a volume called TELEPHONE
POLES and contains another excellent poem,
"Seven Stanzas at Easter," that orginally
appeared in the *Christian Century* and is worth
everyone's reading.

i'm sick, home from school. i'm supposed
to be in bed (that's where jan left me this
morning, filled with aspirin, cold tablets, cough
medicine, plenty of juices, and not one stinking
cigarette — i about went nuts), and now i'm up and
out in the study, digging the Mamas and Papas
on the hifi: monday, monday, so good to me
(and like that: beautiful stuff). people ought to
listen more to rock and roll; it takes a while to
get used to it, but it provides some fascinating
insights into people of my generation, as well as
the kids who are my younger brothers and sisters
and the whole hippy, teeny-bopper world. it's

kind of scary in a way, kind of sad in a way: remembering the Circle this summer and all these kids with hip huggers and wheat jeans; the girls trying to show off breasts they didn't have yet; and all night (literally) the frenzied beat of a pair of congo drums: sex, drugs, music: the whole business merging into this milling mass of up to some 4 or 5 hundred kids—some beautiful things had the possibility of happening—and some downright ugly things: it's a hard world to move with (more about that some other time).

jim and i get together roughly three times a week for lunch or coffee on campus, and the rest of us see each other probably twice a week in some form, manner, or other. we're seeing what happens and digging this whole business of being alive in this thing called creation.

i'll let you taste my wine if i can taste yours.

33

In a little brighter vein I want to share with you some of the exciting and sometimes superficial things that are happening here. Today is one of those beautifully cold days— about 15 degrees colder in the office than outside due to the neglect of our absent landlord. Therefore we're all wearing our coats in the office and hoping that none of the kids will come in until the heat comes back on.

I'd like to share with you some of the story about the 15-year-old who has V. D. I've known her since she was 13 and a core member of one of the few girls' fighting gangs that are left in N. Y. Her family was physically intact, owned their own home. The father

works, and the mother is a housewife. A few
months ago they moved out of the ghetto to
an all-white suburb. There are now three
other younger children in the home—sons of
the father's alcoholic brother whose wife
died 1½ years ago.

When Ellie was in grade school, she acted
out constantly because of the all-white staff.
She saw no reason in obeying "those" people.
She was a smart kid, active and very likable,
but did poorly in school. Starting Junior H. S.,
she acted out even more, hung out with older
kids, fought whenever she had a chance. Last
April she discovered she was pregnant. The
end of May she had a miscarriage. Her mother
took her to court, and on my recommendation
she was sent to a detention house for girls.
At this point she completely rejected me
because "I had failed her." Her month-and-a-
half stay in Youth House provided her much
opportunity to think, and she did. But in fact,
she went in the opposite direction; her attitude
changed from hostility toward the "whites"
to rejection of "Negroes."

When she was released from Youth House,
she immediately came to see me again. She
thanked me for knocking some sense into
her head and said that being in Youth House
had been a good experience. (This is usually
not the case, and most of the time Youth
House does nothing more than promote
more overtly deviant behavior.) She is now
the proud owner of a bleeding ulcer and has
an advanced case of V. D.

But on a much more positive note—she
has one of the most positively sensitive and
creative minds in existence. She is active in
one of the group sessions that I started for
between 12 and 15 other girls with many of
the same problems that she has begun to

34

successfully work out. Her attitude towards people is one of individual assessment — not on any basis of color or status but simply because "they" are people like herself. She has also been able to see herself as an individual who has worth.

And she has a personal commitment towards others, especially if they are going through some of the things she has or if she feels they need to start thinking. She has been instrumental in bringing other kids in that she feels need and would benefit, with intensive help, from the group meetings and/or individual counseling. She hopes to go on for training in some type of social service or teaching. You asked what I hoped for her: to go on as she is, keep growing and questioning while knowing that she will have a rough road to go. She's fighting for honesty and rehumanization; and so far she's winning.

35

What a group! And it scares me to death — perhaps the biggest banner I've been waving since I arrived here — "a power-driven freshman has-been," "individualism, honesty, guts, and offensiveness." I've talked my head off to people last year — I went around gathering up professors who would hear out my zeal over this apathetical, socially oriented, lazy school. I wanted to know what was wrong with this place — and why I felt so alone (oh, and so right and special because at least *I* was aware and at least *I* was sounding off about it).

And now suddenly there is this group — a whole bunch of dynamic, tense, offensive, gutty people who are sounding off; and not only that, they want to act.

Why my fear? I don't know. I think I'm afraid because I sense the wretched motives that have been the power behind my sounding off. I have this damnable pride that makes me want to stand out in front of a group and be special. I want it to look like I'm the only one with true concern — true heart, and right at the center of such a "fine Christian concern" is the brotherhood of all people who have been equally forgiven and therefore must treat each other equally. I want to be singled out. I can get all fired up and spurred on when people tell me how wonderful it is for me to have such zeal.

But now there is this group of people who are members of this "socially oriented" campus — they haven't shunned membership if sororities and fraternities as I have. (I didn't want to go Greek, because I thought I'd look more specially oriented and stand up only for the pure, the intellectual, and the spiritual pursuits on campus.) And they are standing up and marching. My "special" banner and horn-tooting for individualism is getting lost in the crowd. And these people don't simply want the respect and special regard of their fellow students as I have wanted; they want action, for a cause other than themselves.

I feel so ugly, so ashamed. Do I stand for anything more than me? I don't know what to do or how to act. I'm so used to soapbox-climbing simply to be on a pedestal rather than to draw attention away from me and toward the horrid gaps which Christian love is so prone toward. I say, "Love the Negro," and what I mean is: "Love me — love my intensive way of speaking — my intensive facial expressions because I'm special — I'm George, haven't you noticed?"

And now this group wants to act for the Negro and for the misdirected Negro hater, and I feel like a total hypocrite — more apathetic than anyone else — more than any insane Ku Klux Klan member — because I've been all out for me. I've confessed to you because in my pride I've fancied that you've been attracted to my specialness, and this has even bolstered my pride all the more because I admire you. Now I stand naked and ugly. May I beg you to pray for me — please — I need God's Spirit to reorient me out of myself and into His command to be a servant.

36

I can only speak of the city from what I have seen and experienced. Of course this will be entirely different from what other people have to say. I have not been depressed by overwhelming poverty, slums, perversion, rats, filth, etc.

I have seen it, but so what. Everyone is running around spouting all sorts of big opinions on how terrible and different the city is. It, the city, just doesn't exist. One may find people with needs existing in poverty, but the filth is only relative to their state of mind. It only has meaning when one can realize how their actions are being influenced by the poverty. People can be happy living in the city; in the dirt. They can be perfectly well adjusted. I'm all for giving clothes to naked children, establishing free clinics, and feeding hungry people. I also feel it is a vital part of the church to be a social-work organization. But we can not get so caught up in social work; the church must be recognized as the body of Christ, as a spiritual force, and not only a helpful organization inside a community. Any group of do-gooders or the government can accomplish the same thing.

I see the church as an old man that someone is pumping new blood into. No matter how many new ideas of how much blood is pumped into him, he will eventually die without an entire new body. Every part of his body that is not made new will die. His arms and legs and muscles are the new roles of the church (the church as a dynamic community structure is one of the roles), but these members are controlled by a vital new brain, the center of all these actions, a brain that is open and new, one that has not forgotten the old experiences, yet can benefit a great deal from them. The whole body must be dominated by the spirit. The spirit which is fairly splitting the body with freedom, love, honesty, and all the millions of things that must make up the path of God.

I don't know what this new church is or whether or not it could even be called a church as we see it today. Maybe the answer lies in ecumenicalism or maybe in an individual church inside of us all. We cannot dwell on what this new church is; we can only start taking steps towards it, steps that will be many and that will take many years to climb them all.

What I am trying to say is that the church is not exclusively or in the main part a social-work organization, and I wish that people would get on the stick that think that way. We, the church workers, are not here to expound on the rats in the community; we are here to deal with people with needs and the rats if the rats are influencing their physical well-being which is influencing their spiritual well-being, but the rats must be influencing them spiritually.

I feel like part of a chain that must not be broken. I feel that the relationships that I have started must not be stopped when I am gone. I cannot be frustrated, because if I have failed, maybe the person that comes after me that takes over my position will not fail.

37

In the six months Ruth and I have been working together here, we have faced many situations, and because we are so unique, so unusual, we have come a long way in understanding each other—realizing the world of difference between us, yet the same in Christ; and in the people around us in our everyday life. I remember how uneasy she appeared while working with the youth when we first arrived here, how reluctant she was to discipline or speak to the youth, afraid she might do or say something wrong, upsetting them. And all along they tested her authority and patience. Not until she began treating them like she would have any white kid did they sit up and take notice. I don't tiptoe through the tulips with them, then why should Ruth because she's white? There's nothing in the book of rules and fair play that says she has to! Then why do white people shy away? Even the pastor shies away from some situations.

Why is it that I can be invited to a home

for a hot-dog-and-beans supper, when the house is a mess, and put my feet up on the table if I wish, and the best china comes off the shelves for a meal that's fit for a king, the house cleaned from top to bottom, and everybody goes into their little act (putting on faked good manners) when Miss Wendall is invited to dinner? "Now you know Negroes just don't feel right if a white person comes to their house and things aren't right!" says Mrs. Hart, making it her excuse for not having us by for dinner. "I'm always afraid they are going to leave thinking my house is dirty and that I can't keep house or something." "Now, Mrs. Hart, there's no sense in you thinking Ruth is something special. She's not! People keep putting her on a pedestal because she's white. All she wants to do is to get acquainted with people, but they just won't let her. They feel they have to go to extremes to please her, and they don't," says I. "Uh, uh, Robert, I just won't feel right!" says she, and that's that! So Ruth and I make it a point to visit her as often as possible—unannounced.

Why is it that whenever I'm out with Ruth and some friends, I'm suddenly aware of being the only Negro in the many places we visit here—theaters, restaurants, and concert halls? And don't tell me it's because Negroes here can't afford it. The dive joints are too crowded on weekends for that lame excuse. If I never see them, then where are they, what do they do for entertainment—stay at home and watch television? The trouble with too many Negroes today is that they act like the "Emancipation" just happened yesterday instead of happening over a hundred years ago. They act like slaves instead of free people. This city has its well-built psychological racial barrier dividing the city into the Northside—Negro, and Southside—white. Unfortunately, all the fun is located on the Southside. I know there are many people that wouldn't know what a decent theater or restaurant looks like unless they have worked in one. I didn't mean to limit this to just one recreation, but in the churches as well. "We're separate, but one in Christ." Why do Negroes shy away?

My point is this: we don't communicate enough. You don't know enough to trust me, and I can sense it. Then come the unseen barriers, psychological barriers between us. You really don't have the freedom you think you have to move around and circulate. Christ is one thing; a Negro family moving into an all-white neighborhood is, by far, another! The best weapon against this sort of thing is knowledge—through communication: sharing thoughts, dreams, hopes, cigarettes, clothes, and coffee.

38

Today I must share with you, all along the way. It is my day off, and I'm taking a bicycle trip. It's warm and sunny, and for an hour I drove up First Avenue amidst cars and noise. Now I experience another noise—so beautiful—oh, this is a world I love! I entered Central Park, got off the beaten track, and I'm in a forest. I hear birds sing, and the water of a small creek trickling and falling. It's really beautiful music! I see fresh green, and blue sky, and the sun sparkling on the water and me. It sounds like a dream world or one of poetry, but it's real, so real! And I fear

I love it too much—so that all a city can ever hold for me is an entirely opposite kind of excitement and thrill. What a joy to be able to look in every direction and see not buildings, cars, fences, roads—I'll go on now. More soon.

It's 12:30 and I'm in my exact opposite situation—through no choice of my own. I'll have to buy a new tube—at a bicycle shop, and who knows where that is? I'm in the Bronx, nearing my destination: Bronx Botanical Gardens. I'm on about 175th Street. After I left Central Park, I hit Harlem and went right through the center of it, then Spanish Harlem. Then I crossed a bridge over the Harlem or East River. I've been going steadily north, through Bronx. Stopped for lunch—pizza and juice! I've walked over 10 blocks because this tire kept going flat. Now it won't take air.

I've made it. I'm sitting in N. Y. Botanical Gardens under one of the most beautiful trees I have ever seen in my whole life. It's a plum tree—in bloom—and so much in bloom there are blossoms all over the tree. I can hardly begin to describe its beauty. The branches grow outward, gently sweep down and almost touch the ground. It's a very pale pink. It's so full of flowers—that's what really gets me! There are beautiful pines—all shades and varieties. Again the grass is green, and there are scattered petals all over. It reminds me of a painting my grandfather did called "Cherry Blossom Snow." In it were big cherry trees in bloom, and the air was so full of falling petals he called it "Snow." It's weird, going from this to people, city, cars, and back to this. I was thinking of it riding up here. The city is exciting, and the people make it so—it's

fascinating and displays a variety of faces.
But I guess it's because I see the trees and
flowers so little that I tend to go into ecstacy
when I see and feel them. Hope you
understand that in my bubbling enthusiasm
for nature I'm not discounting city and people.

Beyond, behind a pine, there is another
full-blossomed tree. It's a much deeper pink.
I'll have to go see what it is. Let me tell you
what happened with my bicycle. It just had
a piece of glass in it, and the guy was real
nice. He patched the tube and didn't charge.
People are great — odd, different as night and
day. Coming up here I meet his kind, and
I encounter someone who yells at me for
having a bike on a sidewalk in the N. Y.
Gardens. So it takes all kinds. It's near
one-thirty now. Not counting all my stops
it took under 3 hours to get here. Oh, how
I love spring and summer and warmth — and
the chance to be out in this weather!! The
sun — it is so warm! I'm next to the pinker
tree. I got a few blossoms that were lying on
the ground. If they're okay, I'll send 'em along
— then you can throw them away.

I'm going to wander into the conservatory
now.

I've seen the flower show — it's in its dying
days — the layout wasn't near as pretty as it
was in Chicago. I'm sitting in another part
now — like a jungle, and it sure is warm. I'm
under some kind of tree that has fat branches
that grow up and look like they're dead; but
from these are plants growing — like iris or
orchids — miniature ones growing right out
of the trunk — and in bright purples and
oranges. Well, I guess this is it for the
conservatory. Do you know, I'm not tired at all!!

Now it's an understatement — I'm kind of

on the pooped side! Saw a lady selling
pretzels and finally decided I had to stop for
a rest. I came through Bronx, crossed the
river again, this time at 155th Street, and
headed west to the Hudson River. It's awful
windy here and makes the pedaling hard!
But it's quite a view! Saw the George
Washington Bridge and across to New Jersey.
It's hazy now and a bit on the chilly side.
I rode past Riverside Church, the one
Rockefeller built. I'm now at 113th. I think
I'll ride through Central Park again — it's a lot
quieter there.

This has been a day! It sure is an
experience. I won't do it again next week,
but soon. It's all great except that unless
you're in a park or on park-type sidewalks,
it's a real struggle to fight the traffic. You
have to ride in the street, and it is dangerous.
Well, I guess I'm rested, so I'll go on to
Central Park again.

Oh, oh, ah — I feel so good now! Made it
home, collapsed on the couch for a few
minutes, then I took a good bath. I feel so
fresh and so rested. I'm sitting in the office,
feet up, and some Bach cantata on. And right
in front of me are some white iris and yellow
mums I bought yesterday.

It's been a day! It's been so good, and
I'm ready to go to work! I saw so much today,
so many beautiful things and so many unique
contrasts. And I'm glad I could share it with
you. It kind of made it extra special.

Now I'm going to treat myself to supper.

Oh, my face feels real warm — it kind of
has a glow for two reasons: sunburn and
me inside!

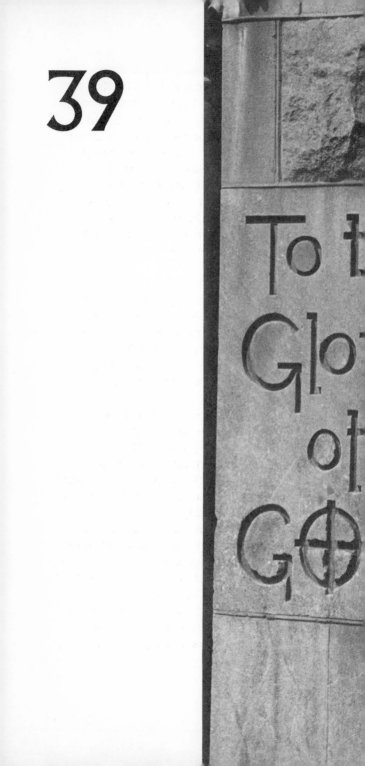

39

To t
Glo
of
G⊕

40

Here in the huge city I don't have
to worry about what the neighbors will
say, because they have removed their
superficiality and dare to be real
"people." In this neighborhood there
are all races, kinds, types, and per-
sonalities. People don't seem to care
what you think. They know that knowing what their neighbor is doing (if
they know their neighbor) doesn't
really matter, and they couldn't care
less what their neighbor thinks about
them. It's great — people aren't doing things for the acceptance of
others — they are doing things for
themselves. Never before have I seen
people so happy with so little. They
seem to be resigned to the idea that
they'll never really be a "success" —
in our terms — but that they can be
happy by doing what they want because
it doesn't matter. Social pressure is
like a malignant disease — it spreads
through all our middle-class minds and
drives us into being what other people
would seemingly like, or notice.
These people have in a sense built up
antibodies against it and are much
healthier. I've made a lot of gen-
eralizations here, but the people I've
met seem this way.

Now I feel like I can find out just
what type of person I really am without all my "friends" and family back

home shaping me. It's a terrific
feeling. It's almost impossible to
describe, though. I'm really God's
child and am just beginning to realize
He loves <u>me</u> — even if I dare to be
myself.

I seem like a different person now.
I think I've grown up more this summer
than in all my 18 years. Life — can
change a person. I just hope and pray
that it's for the better.

41

preparations for christmas proceed apace

and last nite ted and i made schedules and
canceled meetings and when we looked at one
another we prayed and when he danced with
Susan it was a prayer and the lovin' spoonful
asked, "do you believe in magic?" and what
more was there to do than nod

and listened on the telephone for an hour
to a young lady who thinks someone put lsd
in her coffee the day of the kennedy assassination
and she hasn't been straight yet and she is not
very lovable

and mary and i fight and it's a prayer,
a harsh, tough one and ted is there, and mike
is there, tired but there, unaware but there, and
stacey is there with a smile and paul is there
with a calmness and mary is here

and that's a kind of magic, this hereness

and preparations for christ proceed apace

and i can hear mary and stacey singing and
ted is playing the guitar and it's in the basement
that serves as a church (whatever that may be)
and their song is a prayer, a dream, and they
are not afraid to dream the big dream, the
impossible, for every day makes the possible
more terrible, and the wounds are deeper and
in the high-rise someone is hurting, sitting alone
with a drink and dream and we dream different
dreams because he is hurting with his

and she calls again and there is no poetry in
my voice, only a little patience

and it seems a long time until christmas

and i'm standing in the circle and the pigeons
aren't there and it's cold and there is an early
morning mist in the air and the policeman is
wary but assumes a nonchalance and a million
songs are in my head and i know that the figure
of lincoln is brooding over the land and
somewhere in chicago someone is dying and
somewhere in washington one of my pigeons
is dying because the chill mist of death is
heavy in the circle this morning and i'm glad
there is ted and i'm glad there is mike

and it seems a long time until christmas

and mary and stacey are singing about
freedom and we cry a little because so few seem
free from much of everything and "the time has
come" they sing "for peaceful men of peaceful
ways" and they are dying in saigon and hanoi
and chicago and washington and lincoln is
brooding over the land and yesterday ted made
a sign that said "voice your opposition to draft
policies" and we set it up and nine people signed
our petition and it was lonely sitting with the

sign that proclaimed something and someone
asked, "do you want the vietcong to win" and
all i could think was

and it seems a long time until christmas

and seven people from g. w. gather in the
basement for pizza and talk about church music
and someone is stretching out a hand in the
rain and the long black limousines swish down
massachusetts avenue plotting war and a couple
sit in front of the big white house and fast for
peace and in class on tuesday there is a sad
smile on the sorority sister's face and we know
she did it and doesn't know if it was worth it
and she is telling another girl that "this one
started different from all my other love affairs"
and she is maybe eighteen years old

haven't the kings started yet?

it's a long time coming, the talk and the
listening, and it's a strange breed this kind of
life together, over coffee here, a word, a gesture,
a shared dance with mary, buying a new record,
sitting in a meeting with ted, watching mike
eat a weary meal, and we walk our separate
streets sometimes, wondering

haven't the kings started yet?

and it's cold standing here in the circle and
the mist thickens against the morning and it
seems like a different policeman and in our
separate studies we trace our fingers through
the pages of books and sing our songs and
grow our beards

and i know the kings have left, are on their
long, hard way and the early morning mist is

a part of their world and then christmas
doesn't seem so long away

and walking away i pull the collar of my
jacket up a little around my neck and
i remember the prayers, the gestures and the
small squeeze of a hand here and there and
hear mary and stacey and their voices come
through the early morning like the single,
startling note of a bell a long way off and it
seems o. k., the loneliness, the hard times
together, and there is a poem to write when
i get home, a hand to hold and a hot cup
of coffee

and preparations for christmas proceed apace

43

I find it very hard to write this letter. I have
been thinking about what I would say when
the time came for me to leave. While I was
writing a farewell to be put in the church
newspaper, I decided to use 1 Corinthians 13:1:
"I may be able to speak the languages of man
and even of angels, but if I have no love,
then my speech is no more than a noisy gong
or a clanging bell."

When I think of all the talking I have done
this year and all the things I have said, I begin
to wonder just what I did say. Coming from
a middle-class society into the area where
I lived for a year, I had to learn how to talk
all over again. To say "I love you" to a little
child and a pat on the head from me means
nothing. This is what got me thinking all
about the word LOVE, which seems to be
thrown around quite a bit lately.

I had to find out what it meant to love.
I think I learned the hard way. I learned that
to love a little child meant to give up a few
minutes a day to listen to him tell about
school or his problems, that at the time seem
insurmountable, or help him to spell a word
or to read a few simple stories. To love, for
me, was to teach a 5th-grader how to say the
alphabet before we could do his homework.
Loving meant the long subway ride during
the morning rush hour to take John to the eye
doctor once a week. I loved Linette and
Sharon when they came over to the church on
their lunch hour every day to say hi, and also

to put up with their temper tantrums if I paid more attention to one than to the other.

I think I even loved my release-time school class even though they thought the extra hour during the week meant a playtime and at times were enough to drive me up a wall. Love was teaching my Sunday school class to sing "This Little Gospel Light of Mine" and seeing them light up when the time came for them to sing it for their parents. We did a lot of loving during the week when we babysat for children while their mothers went to a discussion group centered in the home and family life.

The kids weren't the only ones we loved this year. Loving was staying with one woman for days while she regained her confidence to face life as it really is and to help her to love her four children. Love was talking to another woman just long enough for her to get her mind off her frustrated life and many children. I loved all the teen-agers that we worked with this summer. I loved them so much it was a task not to get so involved with their lives that there was no room for others. I loved our staff, and with their help and encouragement I was able to love them to the point of a real family. I even loved the sandwiches we ate for one whole year at noon together!

But the whole year was not peaches and cream. There were the times of utter frustration and confusion. We are all human, and we are tempted by noninvolvement and unconcern. It's so much easier for us to say "so what" than it is to say "yes." I remember moving into our apartment and having Sandy and me become the talk of the neighborhood. At first they thought we were prostitutes, then blockbusters, etc.; but when they found out that we were working with one of the local churches, their talk turned to the question why. How could we explain to them that we loved them as people? We weren't there to change their lives from poverty to power, we could do no magic and make the young 17-year-old not have that child. We lived the lives of concerned Christians, and by and by our neighbors saw that we were on the level and accepted us for what we were — people — just like them. We loved them when we lent them our phone, we loved them when we babysat for them, when we went to the doctor with them.

At times I have felt very guilty about being here. I feel that I am taking so much more home with me than I have given out this year. I also feel guilty about having to come to New York City to learn that the same people I knew in Cincinnati are having the same frustrations and problems that these people have. I did learn one thing — it doesn't take poverty to make a person desire love. One man from our congregation said to me that the year I spent here was a waste of time because the church was not filled on a Sunday morning and the Sunday school wasn't overflowing. This was his interpretation of the life I was supposed to live here. Does love really mean filling the church on a Sunday morning? Or does love mean to give yourself to someone who is in need of a little encouragement and let him see by your life that it doesn't take much to love? Do we love by dragging a person out of bed only to sleep in church? Or do we love by first feeding him and then telling him where the food came from? Can we starve a person until he gives in? I don't believe so.

I'll be gone in one week. Or will I? Will I leave behind everything from the kids to our small apartment? I don't think so. I will be taking home with me everything I have learned and everyone I have met. It is a part of me, and there is nothing to separate the two. I grew up here, in just 13 short months. And you can't leave that behind.

44

A lot of my kind of people have a hang-up with the whole church scene. It turns us off. At least I am alienated enough or perhaps free enough to deny to the church's face that it has my God in its little stained-glass box. I refuse to let people use Jesus talk to mask the vacuous content of their thought. Formulas for answers don't work. But I do want and do seek the Word from the very depth of Christian soul, and I want that Word to help me to create a life style. Are you hip to what I'm saying? I do not want to deny historical Christianity or throw away the source of community or turn away from God's radical demands for commitment. I want the church to try, to struggle with seeking God's signs in our times. You dig? That's what it's all about. Like it's not really necessary to go around yelling that God has split the scene and all, but I wish that more people had the vision to express the guts of the Gospel in modern, "secular" human terms, without resorting to tried and true church formulas. Perhaps people raised and steeped in the church tradition are incapable of performing this function. Perhaps we must look to those whose minds have not been inundated from birth with western Judaeo-Christian ethnocentricity to find people who can see more clearly the God of today as well as the God of our fathers.

45

Sweetpea came around right from the time we first opened the PLACE. He came to watch—never taking part in anything, never talking, just standing and listening. We'd always say "hi" when he came in, tell him "so long" when he left, and that was all there was to the relationship. Rarely would he even acknowledge our salutations much less want anything else. By the time a month or two had passed, he would talk, and then he more or less became the life of the party. As Sweetpea became more acclimated to the PLACE, as he came out of his shell (pod?), we noticed there was a sharp upsurge in break-ins during the night. The pattern was always the same, a downstairs window would be broken to gain access, but that would be the only damage. Nothing would ever be damaged, nothing would ever be stolen. All we could tell about the party or parties involved was that they watched t. v. and then pulled some couches together and slept. At first we made no connection between Sweetpea and the break-ins, but soon it became apparent that he was the one involved. Through such comments as "You're kicking me out of my home!" when we were closing, we realized that he had gone from a feeling of total rejection of us and the PLACE to a feeling that it was really his home. He would be here when we opened, be the last to leave when we closed, and then would come back in and spend the night—he thought more of his home (as far as time spent there) than most people ever do—he loved it! Unfortunately, before any further steps could be taken, he was arrested a few weeks ago for grand larceny, and he has been sent up for quite a while. We reached him, but did we do him any good? We think so, but who knows?

Frank is our bad guy. He has been in for attempted murder twice (he has admitted to us once that he did shoot one of them) but was released for insufficient evidence each time. He has served seven jail sentences already, and when we met him, he very casually explained to me, that as far as he was concerned, he had pretty well had it as far as society was concerned, and so why not go down in a blaze of glory? He knew that it was just a matter of time until he got somebody bad, or they got him, so why sweat it? Sure enough, one night in the best tradition of the Old West, some fourteen-year-old kid challenged Frank by throwing a ping-pong paddle at his head. He ducked around the corner and came back with knife out. Before we realized what was happening, he swung the knife at Frank's throat and cut him from one shoulder across his neck to his other shoulder. Luckily, Frank was heavily dressed, and with the exception of a slight knick on

his neck, all it did was slice his clothes open.

We got them pulled apart, and Rita got the young guy in one room, and I had Frank in the big room, trying to persuade him not to murder the kid. He explained that he had been challenged, and he couldn't let the punk get away with that. He was the king, and if he let it slide, every punk in the city would try the same thing, bragging that they had dared to mess with Frank. Frank is the type who has a more or less pat answer for anything, and I was at a loss as to what to do. We could always bring the kid home tonight, but it would just be a matter of time before Frank found him.

Then I noticed that he had a small gold crucifix around his neck. "What's that piece of junk?" I asked him, pointing. He was taken aback and asked me what I meant. "You don't mean a little piece of metal means anything to you, do you?" He got kind of upset and unsure. He knew I was a "church social worker," and this didn't make sense. I continued that if it meant anything at all, how could he talk about murder because some punk had insulted him. If he was going to do what he claimed he was going to do, why not just throw the crucifix in the garbage can or at least give it to someone that it might have real meaning for. Frank probably stood there, looking at me and at the door where the kid was, for three minutes. Then he held out his hand and promised he wouldn't get the kid tonight. More than that he couldn't promise. He needed time to think.

Well, as it worked out, he never did bother the kid, even though everybody knew he had cut at him. Strangely enough, as far as we know, Frank doesn't even carry his knife anymore—at least he has never taken it out, even when he was challenged in a fight where other guys did have them out. He got a job about a month ago and has even cut down on his drinking. Perhaps the most significant proof of change was a week ago, when his 14-year-old cousin was assaulted in the men's room; after going with Rita to take her home, he came back to the PLACE as he promised, rather than going out after the guy, and we all talked for almost an hour. When he left that evening, it was to go and find the guy all right, but not for vengeance. He promised to bring him over to our house, where we could all talk it out. As it worked out, he didn't find the guy that night, but the guy did come over the following morning, and he told us he came because Frank had said I wanted to see him. How much of what was accomplished was in any way attributable to the PLACE is, of course, unknowable. The major point, however, is that a major change has occurred, and if nothing else, we have tried to furnish a locale that will not stifle change.

Who else shall I talk about? Should I mention Eddie and Jean, who had troubles with a pregnancy and parental efforts to force an abortion? How about Big John, who was the one who attempted statutory rape in the men's room? What about Johnnie, who goes out of his way to give Rita a hard time, because he wants to sulk when he is "punished." Eugene is "in love" with Rita (he's serious), even in talking to her. What should I say to him? There are hundreds of kids here, each one with a story they are dying to tell, but each one has to tell it or act it out in his own way. I guess that's what we are doing here — trying to give them all a way and a place to be heard on their own terms. It's great.

With trepidation I leave my typewriter and go back to the PLACE to see if there is anything left standing, to find out if I make it back all right, and to see if there have been any major traumas in my absence.

(EDITOR'S NOTE: A phone call a month after this letter reported that 18-year-old Frank was shot to death, supposedly by his best friend.)

47

"Which project do we go to now? The pink or green—"

"No, the beige one. Yuk!"

"Why 'yuk'? Looks nice from here."

We'd just eaten a big lunch, which was probably a mistake for working in the projects. A fist slams several times on the elevator buttons. They don't work. The whole place seems to be out of order. So we must take the stairs, which wander up twelve flights of dreary apartments. Two of us duck into the entrance and race up the steps, which are dripping wet from the antiseptic used to swab down the halls. It smells like vomit and stale food, though, and filth—filth of society. It's a game. You grab a big breath and run to see how many doors you can knock on before taking another agonizing breath. The consequences aren't pleasant, though, when the smell gets strong. If you lose, you're in danger of losing lunch too.

The door opens. The heat is suffocating; how can anyone stand to live in such heat? Maybe the heating is broken; they don't fix anything around these places.

"Do you have any children between the ages of four and fourteen?" The usual questions begin to tumble out of my mouth. This lady says she has twelve. *Twelve* children in that tiny apartment! The whole idea is nauseating. Low-cost housing with high rent. The only way they keep them low cost is not to keep them up at all. Broken elevators, filthy halls and walls. It's all very depressing. You feel like

crawling up in a corner and crying. God lets
this exist?

The people around here never dress; they
come to the door in slips and bathrobes and
only open the door a crack. Everyone chain-locks
his doors. Guess they're afraid, maybe of life.
Why dress if you never go out? Stay inside all
day in those imprisoning walls. Horrible! Finally
one woman lets you in. The room is dark;
shades are drawn. She remembers the girls from
last year. Real friendly. Obviously she wants
to talk, so you listen. Discovery! These people
are human, not animals. They are only forced
to live that way. You want to hug her. She lets
you in, into *her* society, where middle-class
whites are resented. Canvassing had been sort
of depressing, a drag. But she stirs up excitement,
and you are ready to go on as you step out of
her door.

The halls remind you of a hospital, long,
narrow, sprinkled with numbered doors. Ceiling
lights burn continuously because the halls never
see daylight. The lights bounce off the walls and
give the atmosphere an eerie touch, like walking
in the twilight zone. You pass out of three doors
before you get to the stairs. This place is like
a maze. Imagine getting lost on the way to
your apartment.

You sit in the courtyard and rest while
watching the children play. The pink project
seemed awfully monotonous; the same colored
doors, one after another, and the same-shaped
halls on every floor. But at least it was
somehow well kept. But this beige one was
awful. They get worse as you go. Why go?
You're finished, fed up as far as you are
concerned. There is a gnawing ache down in
your stomach. How could God let such injustice
exist? It's time to go sulk, be depressed, forget

a God who has failed. Don't see any more.
Forget it exists.

As you think about getting up to go, a little
girl runs up, grabs your hands, and shouts, "Let's
go to playday!" You tell her that playdays don't
start for a few days. You see the excitement in
her eyes. She hugs you, and you hug back.
There's a lump in your throat. Like all kids,
these kids need love. They don't even know you;
yet they are willing to express love to you.
Would you do that to a stranger? You eat up
their love and return yours. At last you've
found a place where love can be shared without
hostility and suspicions. Rejoice! This is an
example of God's love. It's time to celebrate
and not be depressed.

SE 6.P.M
AND TIRED
OF TRICKS
WE WAN 6
EACH WEEK IN
VE US
CH DA
R DA
GHT

50

Well, I'm alive, and things are looking good. I never knew I could be so happy about just being alive, but I am. I miss all of you, but I can't depend on you. I have to look to myself. I'm determined not to waste this year; I mean I don't know how many there are left, but I want to live, I mean really live, meeting people, having fun, giving.

I've finally hit on the right relationship with my parents. A lonely one, but I know it's right. It's one that entails nothing deep, not kidding around, not being close, but just being polite and giving them no reason to complain, and living my life to the fullest in all ways. It's working, but I miss them.